THE CARTOON BANK PRESENTS

THE
NEW YORKER
BOOK OF WINE CARTOONS

THE
NEW YORKER
BOOK OF WINE CARTOONS

"Sorry, but you're going to have to remind me who gets
the red wine and who gets the white?"

"*Something drinkable right now.*"

"Oh, Lord! Not another wine-and-cheese party!"

"If it's a California wine you wish, Mr. Larry will assist you."

"*This is a big wine. I recommend you order some big food.*"

*"May I say, sir, the staff and I just knew you'd
see through that Beaujolais."*

"*My compliments, Stefan. Marvelous wine, excellent reception.*"

"It's a little white wine Stuart brought back
from Idaho. Are you game?"

"On second thought, I'll have sangria. I had rosé
the last time we buried the hatchet."

"We go to these things hoping to discover either a terrific new artist or a good, cheap, drinkable California white."

"This one's kerosene, the other's Chardonnay."

"I want Chardonnay, but I like saying 'Pinot Grigio.'"

"And what is your preference in wine—single or double figures?"

"We're hoping for a really smooth wine here."

S.GROSS

"I want to introduce you guys to what I feel is
a really gifted young Zinfandel."

"This is a night for white wine."

"Here's one I know we had before, but I don't
remember if we hated it or loved it."

"Daddy has to clear his head for a few minutes
before he can deal with 'Babar.'"

"What's the right wine to go with severance pay?"

"Who will carry on when I'm gone? All my kids are in recovery."

"*As you may have guessed, Stu, I asked you over tonight for more than just a little wine and cheese.*"

"Wine! Men! Song!"

"The great is $54.99, and I do have a near-great for $23.99."

"We'd love to, but we had too much wine
and cheese in the eighties."

"*Ça suffit, good buddy!*"

"Our best—rated over 700 in both Math and Verbal."

BAR BAR

"Of course, not everybody can face this kind of responsibility."

"Made with pride in our basement."

"You'll notice that I was born in 1968—a very prestigious year."

"More wine! Less truth!"

CHIANTIS IN TRANSLATION

"Village of Overworked Housewives"

Gorgeous Hill Town without Newspapers

Valley Teeming with Abandoned Refrigerators

crawford

"You grab the food—I'll grab the wine."

"And it was a good year for the Mets, too!"

"That's between me and my vintner."

AFTER THE BREAKUP OF
BACCHUS, INC.

Ed, God of Red Wine

Judy, Goddess of White Wine

Charles, God of Rosé

Bobbi Jo, Goddess of Sherry, Port, and Passover-Type Wines

Ray, God of Wine Coolers

r.cht

"Sure, they drank it—but did they get it?"

"This is actually quite good. Remember the first time you tried to order pizza?"

"*That bottle with the little flowers on the label isn't one of those that are going through the roof, is it?*"

"Let me guess. You had it up to here with
the world of business, so you packed it all in and
started your own winery."

"Some wine with your vest?"

"Not much—just flushing out my arteries."

*"Then the demons that drove me to Tangier to try to write fiction turned
around and drove me to the Napa Valley to make wine."*

"*Charles, would you be my vintner?*"

"Barry made the wine. I made the cheese."

"Excellent, but not fit for a king."

"It means taking a hefty pay cut, but I've decided to accept the position as god of wine."

"At your opening, I see that you had two glasses of wine, eight pieces of cheddar, eight crackers, and seventeen grapes. That, of course, will have to come off the top of your end."

"By the way, hon, great food, great wine, great you."

"That will be perfect. We have a lot to talk about."

"Is Pinot Noir where you want to be?"

"It's a naïve domestic Burgundy without any breeding,
but I think you'll be amused by its presumption."

"All of a sudden he can't stand the taste of beer."

"Haven't you ever seen California wine being made before?"

"*You serve an inferior wine, Ted, but you have a nice view of Peconic Bay.*"

"Might I suggest the most expensive wine and the most expensive dinner?"

"It's your friend who writes about wine."

"It's a full-bodied wine with hints of acrimony, partisanship, and moral outrage."

"What do you have in investment-grade reds?"

"We didn't have time to pick up a bottle of wine, but this
is what we would have spent."

"I love these quiet evenings at home battling alcoholism."

"*Our house wine is abominable.*"

"Am I the only guy at this table who goes back to when this stuff was two hundred and fifty dollars a bottle?"

"Hey, Johnny—am I nuts, or does this have a hint of oak?"

"Would you care to see our gasoline list, or do you know what you want?"

"eBay '99."

BOUTIQUE GASOLINES

CHÂTEAU HAUT-SUNOCO 1985

TEXACO CLASSICO 1992

Domaine de Mobil 1997

"A fleshy yet powerful blend, with notes of oak, pepper, coffee, and chocolate."

~ Ed, The Gasoline Spectator

"A fuel of purity and symmetry, revealing a heady aroma of black cherry, licorice, and leather."

~ Gus, Gasoline Enthusiast

"Drivers will enjoy its exotic nose of coconut, plums, and fresh-cut grass."

~Dwayne, Gas and Oil Connoisseur

R. Chst

SIPRESS

"Can you recommend a large-breasted Burgundy with a big behind?"

"We like you better than Robert Mondavi."

SIPRESS

"My approach is nontraditional, but from a uniquely Western perspective."

CRAWFORD

FRENCH ARMY KNIFE

"*Typical trust-fund red from a vanity vintner.*"

"This isn't just any old food wine. This is the foodies' food wine."

"And don't try to pull the old 'good wine steward, bad wine steward' routine."

"Citizen of the world, wine connoisseur, husband. I may be spreading myself too thin."

"And pick up a wine—something that goes with fish."

VINTAGE REMEDIES

"I'm getting a lot of negativity in this one—is it French?"

"Susan, this might be just the wine talking,
but I think I want to order more wine."

INDEX OF ARTISTS